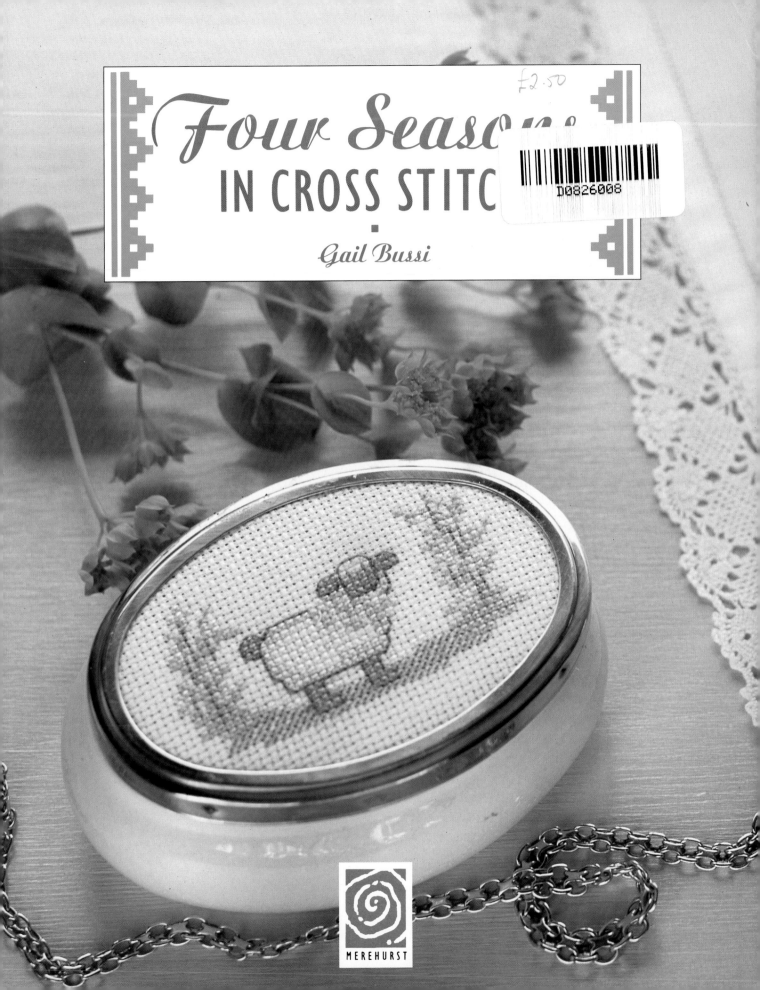

Four Seasons
IN CROSS STITCH

Gail Bussi

£2.50

D0826008

MEREHURST

THE CHARTS

Some of the designs in this book are very detailed and due to inevitable space limitations, the charts may be shown on a comparatively small scale; in such cases, readers may find it helpful to have the particular chart with which they are currently working enlarged.

THREADS

The projects in this book were all stitched with DMC stranded cotton embroidery threads. The keys given with each chart also list thread combinations for those who wish to use Anchor or Madeira threads. It should be pointed out that the shades produced by different companies vary slightly, and it is not always possible to find identical colours in a different range.

First published in 1995 by Merehurst Limited
Ferry House, 51-57 Lacy Road, Putney, London SW15 1PR
Text, photography & illustrations © Copyright 1994 Merehurst Limited
ISBN 1 85391 441 X
Reprinted 1995

A catalogue record for this book is available from the British Library.

Commissioning Editor Cheryl Brown
Edited by Diana Lodge
Designed by Maggie Aldred
Photography by Marie-Louise Avery
Illustrations by John Hutchinson
Typesetting by Dacorum Type & Print, Hemel Hempstead
Colour separation by Fotographics Limited, UK – Hong Kong
Printed in Hong Kong by Wing King Tong

Merehurst is the leading publisher of craft books and has an excellent range of titles to suit all levels. Please send to the address above for our free catalogue, stating the title of this book.

CONTENTS

INTRODUCTION

The four seasons – each with their unique features and own special beauty – remind us of the natural cycles and rhythms of our world and provide us with an ever-changing panorama of colours, sights and sounds.

Seasonal images have long been a favourite theme in many creative arts, such as painting, quilting and various kinds of embroidery. In this book you will find seasonal designs specially created with the cross stitcher in mind.

Whatever your level of skill – whether you are an experienced cross stitcher or relatively new to this popular pastime – you are sure to enjoy creating one or more of these designs, either as a lovely gift or as something special to grace your home. There are a number of different projects, ranging from special pictures celebrating each of the four seasons to an autumn harvest tray, a festive sampler and summery roses stitched on table linen.

So enjoy the book, and may you experience the pleasure of creating a handstitched design that echoes the seasonal patterns of our beautiful world.

BASIC SKILLS

■

BEFORE YOU BEGIN

PREPARING THE FABRIC

Even with an average amount of handling, many evenweave fabrics tend to fray at the edges, so it is a good idea to overcast the raw edges, using ordinary sewing thread, before you begin.

FABRIC

Some projects in this book use Aida fabric, which is ideal both for beginners and more advanced stitchers as it has a surface of clearly designated squares. All Aida fabric has a count, which refers to the number of squares (each stitch covers one square) to one inch (2.5cm); the higher the count, the smaller the finished stitching. Other projects in this book use either 14- or 18-count Aida, two popular and readily available sizes, in a wide variety of colours. Linen has been used for several projects in this book; although less simple to stitch on than Aida fabric (because you need to count over a specified number of threads) it does give a very attractive, traditional finish. The most commonly available linen has 28 threads to 2.5cm (1in), which when worked over two threads gives a stitch count of 14 to 2.5cm (1in).

THE INSTRUCTIONS

Each project begins with a full list of the materials that you will require. The measurements given for the embroidery fabric include a minimum of 5cm (2in) all around to allow for stretching it in a frame and preparing the edges to prevent them from fraying.

Colour keys for stranded embroidery cottons – DMC, Anchor or Madeira – are given with each chart. It is assumed that you will need to buy one skein of each colour mentioned in a particular key, even though you may use less, but where two or more skeins are needed, this information is included in the main list of requirements.

To work from the charts, particularly those where

several symbols are used in close proximity, some readers may find it helpful to have the chart enlarged so that the squares and symbols can be seen more easily. Many photocopying services will do this for a minimum charge.

Before you begin to embroider, always mark the centre of the design with two lines of basting stitches, one vertical and one horizontal, running from edge to edge of the fabric, as indicated by the arrows on the charts.

As you stitch, use the centre lines given on the chart and the basting threads on your fabric as reference points for counting the squares and threads to position your design accurately.

WORKING IN A HOOP

A hoop is the most popular frame for use with small areas of embroidery. It consists of two rings, one fitted inside the other; the outer ring usually has an adjustable screw attachment so that it can be tightened to hold the stretched fabric in place. Hoops are available in several sizes, ranging from 10cm (4in) in diameter to quilting hoops with a diameter of 38cm (15in). Hoops with table stands or floor stands attached are also available.

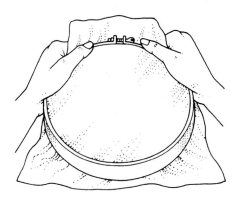

1 To stretch your fabric in a hoop, place the area to be embroidered over the inner ring and press the outer ring over it, with the tension screw released. Tissue paper can be placed between the outer ring and the embroidery, so that the hoop does not mark the fabric. Lay the tissue paper over the fabric when you set it in the hoop, then tear away the central embroidery area.

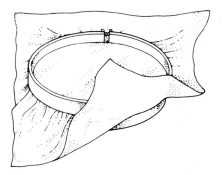

2 Smooth the fabric and, if necessary, straighten the grain before tightening the screw. The fabric should be evenly stretched.

WORKING IN A RECTANGULAR FRAME

Rectangular frames are more suitable for larger pieces of embroidery. They consist of two rollers, with tapes attached, and two flat side pieces, which slot into the rollers and are held in place by pegs or screw attachments. Available in different sizes, either alone or with adjustable table or floor stands, frames are measured by the length of the roller tape, and range in size from 30cm (12in) to 68cm (27in).

As alternatives to a slate frame, canvas stretchers and the backs of old picture frames can be used. Provided there is sufficient extra fabric around the finished size of the embroidery, the edges can be turned under and simply attached with drawing pins (thumb tacks) or staples.

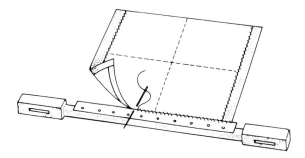

1 To stretch your fabric in a rectangular frame, cut out the fabric, allowing at least an extra 5cm (2in) all around the finished size of the embroidery. Baste a single 12mm (½in) turning on the top and bottom edges and oversew strong tape, 2.5cm (1in) wide, to the other two sides. Mark the centre line both ways with basting stitches. Working from the centre outward and using strong thread, oversew the top and bottom edges to the roller tapes. Fit the side pieces into the slots, and roll any extra fabric on one roller until the fabric is taut.

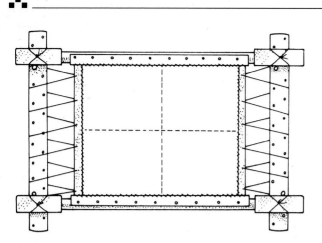

2 Insert the pegs or adjust the screw attachments to secure the frame. Thread a large-eyed needle (chenille needle) with strong thread or fine string and lace both edges, securing the ends around the intersections of the frame. Lace the webbing at 2.5cm (1in) intervals, stretching the fabric evenly.

EXTENDING EMBROIDERY FABRIC

It is easy to extend a piece of embroidery fabric, such as a bookmark, to stretch it in a hoop.

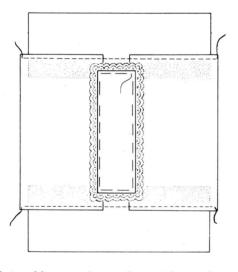

● Fabric oddments of a similar weight can be used. Simply cut four pieces to size (in other words, to the measurement that will fit both the embroidery fabric and your hoop) and baste them to each side of the embroidery fabric before stretching it in the hoop in the usual way.

MOUNTING EMBROIDERY

The cardboard should be cut to the size of the finished embroidery, with an extra 6mm (¼in) added all round to allow for the recess in the frame.

LIGHTWEIGHT FABRICS

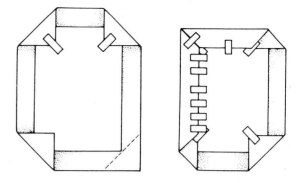

1 Place embroidery face down, with the cardboard centred on top, and basting and pencil lines matching. Begin by folding over the fabric at each corner and securing it with masking tape.

2 Working first on one side and then the other, fold over the fabric on all sides and secure it firmly with pieces of masking tape, placed about 2.5cm (1in) apart. Also neaten the mitred corners with masking tape, pulling the fabric tightly to give a firm, smooth finish.

HEAVIER FABRICS

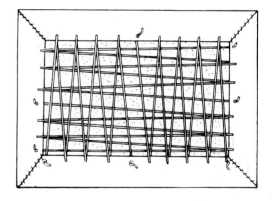

● Lay the embroidery face down, with the cardboard centred on top; fold over the edges of the fabric on opposite sides, making mitred folds at the corners, and lace across, using strong thread. Repeat on the other two sides. Finally, pull up the fabric firmly over the cardboard. Overstitch the mitred corners.

CROSS STITCH

For all cross stitch embroidery, the following two methods of working are used. In each case, neat rows of vertical stitches are produced on the back of the fabric.

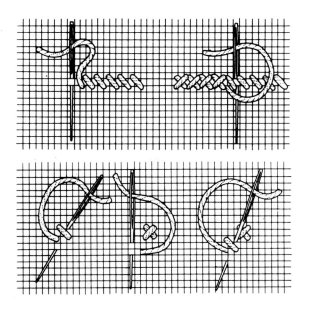

• When stitching large areas, work in horizontal rows. Working from right to left, complete the first row of evenly spaced diagonal stitches over the number of threads specified in the project instructions. Then, working from left to right, repeat the process. Continue in this way, making sure each stitch crosses in the same direction.

• When stitching diagonal lines, work downwards, completing each stitch before moving to the next. When starting a project always begin to embroider at the centre of the design and work outwards to ensure that the design will be placed centrally on the fabric.

BACKSTITCH

Backstitch is used in the projects to give emphasis to a particular foldline, an outline or a shadow. The stitches are worked over the same number of threads as the cross stitch, forming continuous straight or diagonal lines.

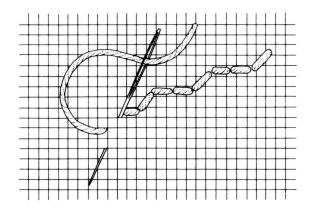

• Make the first stitch from left to right; pass the needle behind the fabric and bring it out one stitch length ahead to the left. Repeat and continue in this way along the line.

THREE-QUARTER CROSS STITCHES
Some fractional stitches are used on certain projects in this book; although they strike fear into the hearts of less experienced stitchers they are not difficult to master, and give a more natural line in certain instances. Should you find it difficult to pierce the centre of the Aida block, simply use a sharp needle to make a small hole in the centre first.

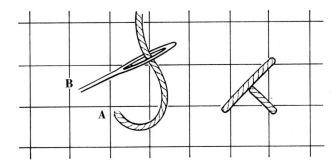

To work a three-quarter cross, bring the needle up at point A and down through the centre of the square at B. Later, the diagonal back stitch finishes the stitch. A chart square with two different symbols separated by a diagonal line requires two 'three-quarter' stitches. Backstitch will later finish the square.

A clear distinction needs to be made between three-quarter stitches and half cross stitches, which have been used in a number of projects in this book. A three-quarter stitch occupies half of a square diagonally. A half cross stitch is like a normal cross stitch, but only the top stitch is worked, to give a more delicate effect. Stitches worked in this way are indicated quite clearly on the colour keys with their own symbols.

Promise of Spring

Daffodils, violets, delicate primroses
and a spring bunny – all of these
evoke spring, the freshest of the
seasons, with its promise of new life.
This is the first of four similar
seasonal pictures in this book, and it
would look delightful in any setting.

PROMISE OF SPRING

YOU WILL NEED

For the *Spring* picture, set in a mount with a cut-out measuring 12.5cm × 16cm (5in × 6¼in):

*32.5cm × 36cm, (13in × 14¼in) of antique white, 18-count Aida fabric
Stranded embroidery cotton in the colours given in the panel
No26 tapestry needle
Wooden frame measuring 22.5cm × 26cm (8¾in × 10¼in)
Rectangular mount, cut to fit the frame, with cut-out as specified above
Strong thread and cardboard, for mounting*

•

THE EMBROIDERY

Prepare the fabric as described on page 4; find the centre by folding, and mark the horizontal and vertical centre lines with basting stitches in a light-coloured thread. Set the fabric in a frame or hoop (see page 5) and count out from the centre to start stitching at a point convenient to you.

One thread of cotton was used in the needle for cross stitches and for backstitch. Work all full cross stitches first, and then the half crosses. The half cross stitches have their own individual symbols on the chart; for each half cross, work only the top stitch of the two that make up a full cross stitch, to produce a more delicate effect.

Take both half and full crosses over one block of the fabric, making sure that all top stitches run in the same direction (if top stitches run in different directions, they will reflect the light in opposite directions and the work will look uneven). Finally, work all backstitch details.

FINISHING

Gently handwash the finished piece, if necessary, and lightly press with a steam iron on the wrong side. Stretch and mount the embroidery as explained on page 6. Insert it into the frame, behind the rectangular mount.

For each of these seasonal pictures, the colour of the mount has been specially selected to echo colours and tones predominant in that particular design, but if you are making them as a set, you might prefer to use one colour for all four.

TOP

PROMISE OF SPRING ▲			DMC	ANCHOR	MADEIRA
Cross	**Half Cross**				
•		Very light mauve	3743	869	0801
O		Light antique mauve	3042	870	0807
▲		Medium antique mauve	3041	871	0806
X		Medium yellow	744	301	0112
S		Medium grey-green	522	860	1513
V	/	Very light grey-green	524	858	1511
−		Light yellow	745	300	0111
△		Medium gold	725	305	0108
■		Light orange	402	1047	2307

10

	Cross	Half Cross	DMC	ANCHOR	MADEIRA
●		Medium brownish green	3052	859	1509
C		Light yellow green	3364	266	1501
		Dark golden brown*	611	898	2107
B		Medium golden brown	612	832	2108
T		Light golden brown	613	831	2109
P		Pale shell pink	3713	48	0502
	I	Light grass green	471	266	1501
U		White	White	2	White
M		Pale cream	822	390	1908

	Cross	Half Cross	DMC	ANCHOR	MADEIRA
		Medium khaki*	370	855	2112
\		Light khaki	372	853	2110
		Medium cornflower blue*	794	175	0907
	L	Very light cornflower blue	3747	120	1002

Note: backstitch the border outline in medium khaki*, the violets and bunny in dark brown* and the lines on the sky in medium cornflower blue* (starred outline colours are not indicated by symbols on the chart). The bunny's eye is stitched with a half cross in dark golden brown*

Spring Creatures

These delightful designs feature a goose and lamb, both surrounded by spring flowers; they have been made up as gift items in small porcelain and glass boxes, but would also make wonderful Easter cards or small pictures for childrens' rooms.

SPRING CREATURES

YOU WILL NEED

For the *Goose with violets*, set in a frosted glass bowl, 7.5cm (3in) in diameter:

15cm (6in) square of white, 18-count Aida fabric
Stranded embroidery cotton in the colours given
in the panel
No26 tapestry needle
Frosted glass bowl (for suppliers, see page 48)

For the *Lamb with blossoms*, set in an oval porcelain box, 8cm (3¼in) long:

15cm (6in) square of pale pink, 18-count Aida fabric
Stranded embroidery cotton in the colours given
in the panel
No26 tapestry needle
Pale pink oval porcelain box
(for suppliers, see page 48)

NOTE: If you are stitching both designs, you will only require one skein of each of the colours listed.

•

THE EMBROIDERY

For each design, prepare the fabric, marking the centre of the design with horizontal and vertical lines of basting stitches in a light-coloured thread. You can either set the fabric in a hoop or, for these small-scale designs, hold the work in the hand as you embroider. Start the embroidery from the centre and work outwards, working the cross stitches first and then finishing with the backstitching. Use one strand of embroidery cotton in the needle for both cross stitches and backstitching.

Wash the finished embroidery, if necessary, and lightly press with a steam iron. It is a good idea to leave the basting stitches in at this stage, as they will prove useful in helping you to centre your design in the lid.

ASSEMBLING THE LID

Place the finished embroidery face up on a firm, flat surface. Gently remove all parts from the lid of the trinket box. Use the rim of the lid and the basting stitches to centre the design. Using a hard pencil, draw a line on the fabric, around the outer edge of the lid, then cut along the drawn line, trimming the fabric to shape. Remove the basting stitches.

To assemble the lid, replace the clear acetate and place your design in the lid, with the right side to the acetate. Place the sponge behind your design. Push the metal locking disc very firmly into place, using thumb pressure, with the raised side of the disc facing the sponge. When the locking disc is tightly in position, use a little glue to secure the flock lining card to it.

GOOSE WITH VIOLETS ▶			DMC	ANCHOR	MADEIRA
Cross	Half Cross				
M		Mauve	554	96	0711
•		White	White	2	White
/		Very light grey	762	397	1804
X	\	Very light grey green	524	858	1511
P		Medium salmon pink	761	8	0404
O		Light pink	3713	48	0502
L		Light orange	402	1047	2307
Y		Light yellow	745	300	0111
		Medium grey green*	522	860	1513
		Medium orange*	722	323	0307
		Dark grey*	414	235	1801

Note: backstitch the stems on the wreath in medium grey green, the feet of the goose in medium orange* and the goose outline in dark grey* (starred colours are used for backstitch only).*

LAMB WITH BLOSSOMS ▶			DMC	ANCHOR	MADEIRA
Cross	Half Cross				
•		White	White	2	White
/		Very light grey	762	397	1804
X		Medium grey	318	399	1802
	I	Medium grey green	522	860	1513
P		Medium salmon pink	761	8	0404
Y		Light yellow	745	300	0111
S		Very light grey green	524	858	1511
		Dark grey*	414	235	1801

Note: backstitch the lamb outline in dark grey (used for backstitch only), and the flower stems in medium grey green.*

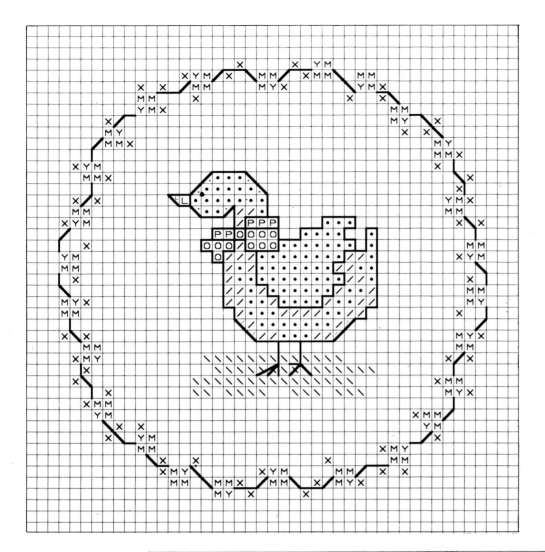

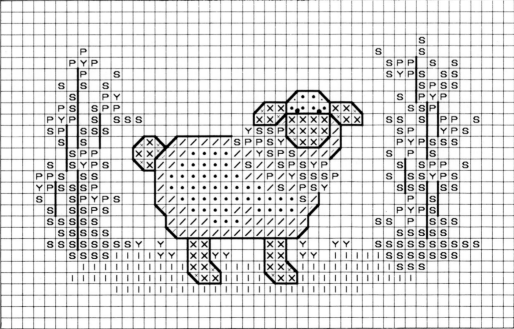

A Touch of Summer

The summer garden is a riot of colour and fragrance, attracting natural visitors, such as brightly-coloured butterflies; the summer flowers and fruit at the front of this design lead the eye to the view of a cottage garden behind, complete with a rose-covered arch.

A TOUCH OF SUMMER

YOU WILL NEED

For the *Summer* picture, set in a mount with a cut-out measuring 12.5cm × 16cm (5in × 6¼in):

32.5cm × 36cm (13in × 14¼in) of antique white, 18-count Aida fabric
Stranded embroidery cotton in the colours given in the panel
No26 tapestry needle
Wooden frame measuring 22.5cm × 26cm (8¾in × 10¼in)
Rectangular mount, cut to fit the frame, with cut-out as specified above
Strong thread and cardboard, for mounting

•

THE EMBROIDERY

Prepare the fabric as described on page 4; find the centre by folding, and mark the horizontal and vertical centre lines with basting stitches in a light-coloured thread. Set the fabric in a frame or hoop

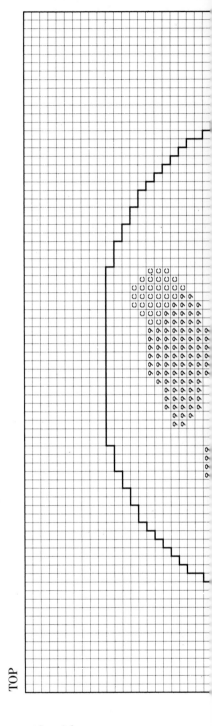

TOP

A TOUCH OF SUMMER ▶			DMC	ANCHOR	MADEIRA
Cross	Half Cross				
•		White	White	2	White
−		Very light pink	819	271	0501
O		Pale shell pink	3713	48	0502
P		Light salmon pink	761	8	0404
▲		Medium salmon pink	760	9	0405
Y		Medium yellow	744	301	0112
C		Light yellow	745	300	0111
B	/	Light golden brown	613	831	2109
		Dark golden brown*	611	898	2107
●		Clear green	3363	262	1602
L		Medium grey green	522	860	1513
V	\	Very light grey green	524	858	1511
S		Light khaki	372	853	2110
■		Medium olive green	3052	859	1509
R		Light olive green	3053	844	1510
6		Light cornflower blue	794	175	0907
△		Medium cornflower blue	793	176	0906
X		Apple green	368	240	1310
8		Medium khaki	370	855	2112
U		Light grass green	471	253	1414
=		Dark pink	3712	1023	0406
∅		Light orange	402	1047	2307
▼		Dark golden brown	611	898	2107
	9	Very pale blue	3753	1031	1001
		Dark grey*	646	815	1809

Note: backstitch the border outline in clear green, fence in dark grey, and strawberry flowers, daisies and butterfly in dark golden brown* (starred outline colours are not indicated by symbols on the chart). Using dark golden brown, make either tiny stitches or french knots to form the dots in the wings and feelers of the butterfly.*

(see page 5) and count out from the centre to start stitching at a point convenient to you.

One thread of cotton was used in the needle for cross stitches and for backstitch. Work all full cross stitches first, and then the half crosses. The half cross stitches have their own individual symbols on the chart; for each half cross, work only the top stitch of the two that make up a full cross stitch, to produce a more delicate effect.

Take both half and full crosses over one block of

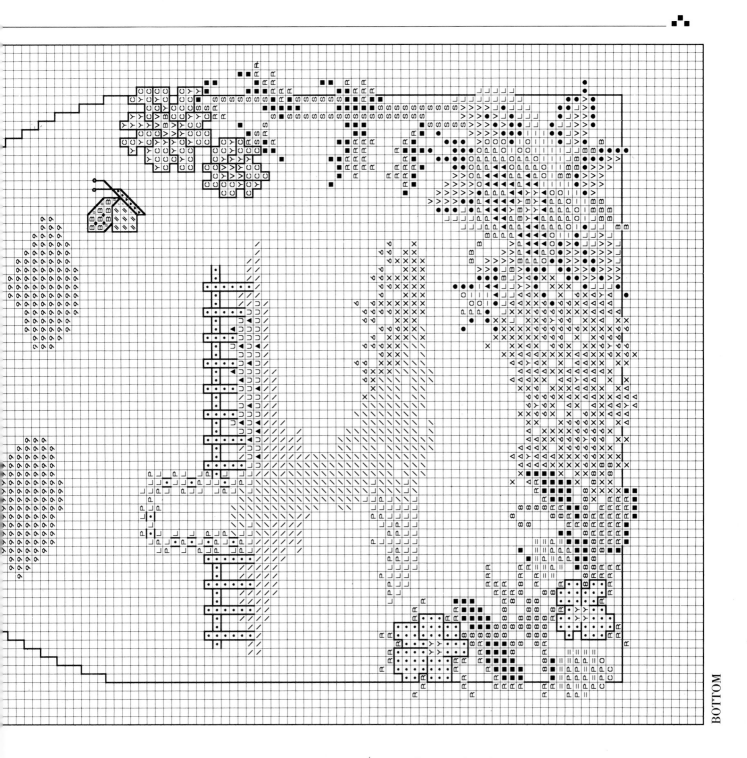

the fabric, making sure that all top stitches run in the same direction (if top stitches run in different directions, they will reflect the light in opposite directions and the work will look uneven). Finally, work all backstitch details.

FINISHING

Gently handwash the finished piece, if necessary, and lightly press with a steam iron on the wrong side. Stretch and mount the embroidery as explained on page 6. Insert it into the frame, behind the rectangular mount.

For each of these seasonal pictures, the colour of the mount has been specially selected to echo colours and tones predominant in that particular design, but if you are making them as a set, you might prefer to use one colour for all four.

The Roses of Summer

If one flower symbolizes the beauty, warmth and brightness of summer it surely must be the rose – the queen of all flowers. In these designs, three different roses have been stitched on purchased tablelinen, creating a table setting that evokes the spirit of summer, even in winter!

THE ROSES OF SUMMER

YOU WILL NEED

For either the *Pink Rose* or *Peach Rose* tablemats,
each measuring 32.5cm × 47.5cm (13in × 19in),
or the *Salmon Pink Rose* napkin, measuring
37.5cm (15in) square:

*Stranded embroidery cotton in the colours given
in the appropriate panel
No24 tapestry needle
Sal-Em 26-count white tablelinen
(for suppliers, see page 48)*

●

THE EMBROIDERY

In each case, start by determining where you are
going to position your chosen design. Choose a
placement that looks balanced to the eye. You may
find that it is helpful to make a line of basting
stitches to mark the outer perimeter of the design;
you can then count inwards to a point where it is
convenient to start stitching.

For each design, make the stitches over two
threads of the linen, using two strands of cotton in
the needle. Make sure that all top crosses face in the
same direction.

When you have completed the stitching, wash the
finished piece, if necessary (Sal-Em tablelinens are
fully washable). Lightly press the embroidered
tablemat or napkin on the wrong side.

PEACH ROSE ▼		DMC	ANCHOR	MADEIRA
•	Very light peach	948	1011	0306
X	Light peach	3779	868	0304
O	Peach	758	0403	9575
●	Dark peach	3778	1013	0303
B	Dark golden brown	611	898	2107
L	Very light grey green	524	858	1511
S	Medium khaki green	3053	844	1510
■	Dark khaki green	3051	681	1508

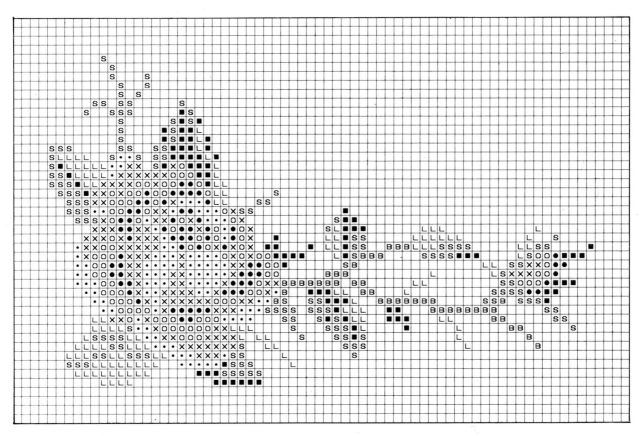

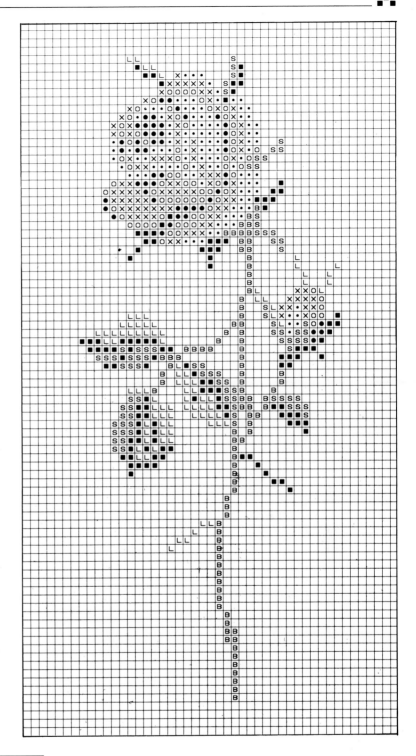

SALMON PINK ROSE ▲	DMC	ANCHOR	MADEIRA
• Shell pink	3713	48	0502
X Light salmon pink	761	8	0404
O Medium salmon pink	760	9	0405
● Dark salmon pink	3712	1023	0406
B Dark golden brown	611	898	2107
L Medium khaki green	3053	844	1510
S Clear green	3363	262	1602

PINK ROSE ▶	DMC	ANCHOR	MADEIRA
• Very pale pink	819	271	0501
X Shell pink	3713	48	0502
O Light dusky pink	224	893	0813
● Medium dusky pink	223	895	0812
B Dark golden brown	611	898	2107
L Very light grey green	524	858	1511
S Light yellow green	3364	266	1501
■ Medium yellow green	3346	267	1407

Seaside Garden Cushion

Sunkissed waves, a wide blue sky, endless golden sands, flowers and grasses blown by sea breezes – the ingredients for a perfect summer's day, are captured here in cross stitch.

SEASIDE GARDEN CUSHION

YOU WILL NEED

For the *Summer Garden* cushion, with an
embroidered area measuring 13.5cm × 10cm
(5⅜in × 4in) on cushion cover measuring
35cm (14in) square:

25cm × 30cm (10in × 12in) of pale blue,
14-count Aida fabric
Stranded embroidery cotton in the colours
given in the panel
No24 tapestry needle
Purchased cushion with removable pad and a cover
approximately 36cm (14in) square
Matching and contrasting sewing threads

•

THE EMBROIDERY

Prepare the fabric as described on page 4; find the
centre by folding, and mark the horizontal and
vertical centre lines with basting stitches in a light-
coloured thread. Set the fabric in a hoop or frame
(see page 5) and count out from the centre to start
stitching at a point convenient to you.

Use two strands of embroidery cotton in the
needle for cross stitches, and take each stitch over
one block of the fabric. Finish with the backstitch
details, using one strand of embroidery cotton.

Wash the finished embroidery, if necessary, and
press lightly on the wrong side with a steam iron.

FINISHING

Carefully trim the fabric to within 4cm (1½in) of the
border line on all sides. Fold a 12mm (½in) hem to
the wrong side all around the embroidery, mitring
the corners (see page 6). Baste the hem in place,
using sewing thread of a contrasting colour and
stitching about 6mm (¼in) in from the folded edge.
Press the piece lightly once again.

Remove the pad from the cushion cover and
carefully pin the prepared embroidery to the centre
of the cover front. Stitch the embroidery in place,
using a matching thread and taking tiny, invisible
stitches (take care not to stitch through both layers
of the cushion cover).

Finally, remove the basting stitches; press the
cushion cover lightly, and re-insert the pad.

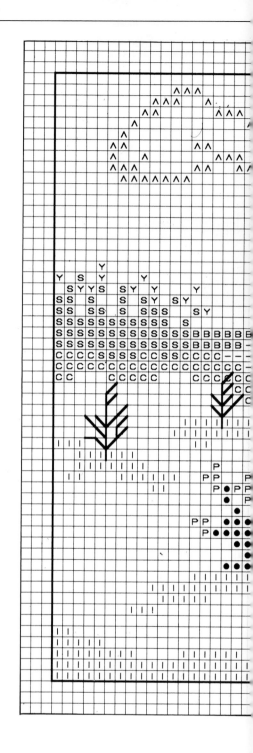

SEASIDE GARDEN ▲

			DMC	ANCHOR	MADEIRA
Cross	Half Cross				
C		Medium blue green	502	876	1703
T		Medium tan brown	435	1046	2010
S		Medium khaki green	3052	859	1509
Y		Light yellow	745	300	0111
	X	Light golden tan	738	361	2013
	/	Very light golden tan	739	366	2014
	I	Light tan brown	437	362	1903
	•	Very light blue	3753	1031	1001
	−	Light blue	3752	1032	1002
	B	Medium antique blue	932	1033	1710

			DMC	ANCHOR	MADEIRA
Cross	Half Cross				
P		Medium peach pink	3779	868	2313
M		Medium mauve	3042	870	0807
U		Light grey green	524	858	1511
•		Light khaki green	3053	844	1510
	∧	White	White	2	White
		Dark khaki green*	3051	846	1508
		Dark antique blue*	930	922	1712

Note: backstitch the grasses in dark khaki green* and the border outline in dark antique blue* (starred colours are used for backstitch only).

Autumn Harvest Tray

The fruits of autumn in all their abundance and rich colourings are vividly portrayed on this stitched piece, which has been made up in the form of a tray. Used throughout the year, it reminds us of earth's bounty and blessings.

AUTUMN HARVEST TRAY

For the tray, measuring 24cm (9½in) square:

*37.5cm (15in) square of 14-count,
Fiddler's Lite Aida fabric
Stranded embroidery cotton in the colours
given in the panel
No24 tapestry needle
Wooden tray (for suppliers, see page 48)*

●

THE EMBROIDERY

Prepare the fabric as described on page 4; find the centre by folding, and mark the horizontal and vertical centre lines with basting stitches in a light-coloured thread. Set the fabric in a frame or hoop and count out from the centre to start stitching at a point convenient to you.

Two threads of cotton were used in the needle for cross stitches and one for backstitching. Work all cross stitches first, taking them over one block of fabric. Make sure that all top stitches run in the same direction. Finally, work all backstitch details.

Remove the embroidery from the frame, and, if necessary, wash gently and then lightly steam press on the wrong side. Do not remove the basting stitches at this stage.

ASSEMBLING THE TRAY

Using a soft pencil, mark the mounting card supplied with the tray horizontally and vertically across the centre. Place the embroidery face down with the card on top, basting and pencil lines matching.

Fold the fabric over at each corner, securing it with masking tape. Working on one side and then the opposite side, fold over the edges of the fabric on all sides and secure with pieces of masking tape. Check to see that the embroidery is centred; if not, simply release the masking tape and readjust the position. Neaten the corners by folding them over to form a mitre (see page 6), and secure with masking tape. Carefully remove basting stitches.

Insert the mounted embroidery into the tray, using the glass and backing boards provided and following the manufacturer's instructions.

AUTUMN HARVEST ▶	DMC	ANCHOR	MADEIRA
X Light grey green	523	859	1512
● Pink red	3328	1024	0406
P Medium salmon pink	760	9	0405
/ Light salmon pink	761	8	0404
G Clear green	3363	262	1602
Dark tan brown*	433	359	2304
O Medium tan brown	435	371	2303
T Light tan brown	437	362	2012
L Medium gold	676	891	2208
M Medium purple	553	98	0712
– Light purple	554	96	0711
▲ Dark yellow green	3051	681	1508
I Light straw	3047	852	2205
S Medium straw	3046	887	2206
U Khaki green	370	855	2112
A Apple green	368	261	1310
B Medium golden brown	612	832	2108
C Medium orange	722	323	0307
\ Light orange	402	1047	2307
Y Medium yellow	744	301	0112
• Light gold	677	886	2205
■ Dark tan	420	374	2104

Note: backstitch the basket outline, the fruit stems and wheatsheaf in dark tan brown* (used for backstitch only) and the outer line and flourishes in clear green.

Autumn Glories

Everywhere in this design there is evidence of the earth's rich abundance and the harvest at the end of the year. Vivid autumnal colours offset the darkening sky, with migrating birds etched against the clouds.

AUTUMN GLORIES

YOU WILL NEED

For the *Autumn* picture, set in a mount with a cut-out measuring 12.5cm × 16cm (5in × 6¼in):

32.5cm × 36cm (13in × 14¼in) of antique white, 18-count Aida fabric
Stranded embroidery cotton in the colours given in the appropriate panel
No26 tapestry needle
Wooden frame measuring 22.5cm × 26cm (8¾in × 10¼in)
Rectangular mount, cut to fit the frame, with cut-out as specified above
Strong thread and cardboard, for mounting

●

THE EMBROIDERY

Prepare the fabric as described on page 4; find the centre by folding, and mark the horizontal and vertical centre lines with basting stitches in a light-coloured thread. Set the fabric in a frame or hoop (see page 5) and count out from the centre to start stitching at a point convenient to you.

One thread of cotton was used in the needle for cross stitches and for backstitch. Work all full cross stitches first, and then the half crosses. The half cross stitches have their own individual symbols on the chart; for each half cross, work only the top stitch of the two that make up a full cross stitch, to produce a more delicate effect.

Take both half and full crosses over one block of the fabric, making sure that all top stitches run in the same direction (if top stitches run in different directions, they will reflect the light in opposite directions and the work will look uneven). Finally, work all backstitch details.

FINISHING

Gently handwash the finished piece, if necessary, and lightly press with a steam iron on the wrong side. Stretch and mount the embroidery as explained on page 6. Insert it into the frame, behind the rectangular mount.

For each of these seasonal pictures, the colour of the mount has been specially selected to echo colours and tones predominant in that particular design, but if you are making them as a set, you might prefer to use one colour for all four.

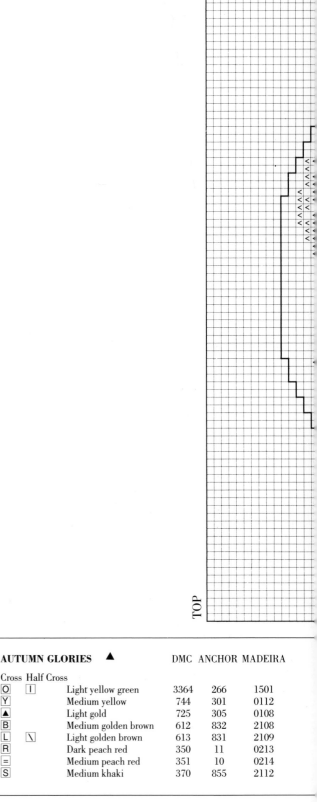

TOP

AUTUMN GLORIES ▲			DMC	ANCHOR	MADEIRA
Cross	Half Cross				
O	I	Light yellow green	3364	266	1501
Y		Medium yellow	744	301	0112
▲		Light gold	725	305	0108
B		Medium golden brown	612	832	2108
L	\	Light golden brown	613	831	2109
R		Dark peach red	350	11	0213
=		Medium peach red	351	10	0214
S		Medium khaki	370	855	2112

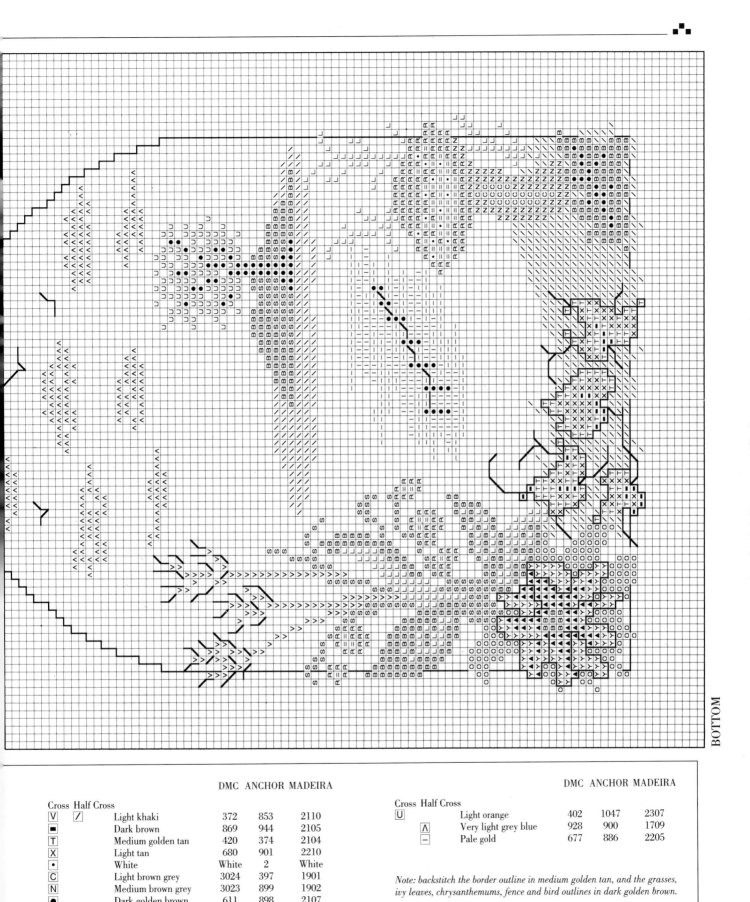

BOTTOM

Cross	Half Cross		DMC	ANCHOR	MADEIRA
V	/	Light khaki	372	853	2110
■		Dark brown	869	944	2105
T		Medium golden tan	420	374	2104
X		Light tan	680	901	2210
•		White	White	2	White
C		Light brown grey	3024	397	1901
N		Medium brown grey	3023	899	1902
●		Dark golden brown	611	898	2107

Cross	Half Cross		DMC	ANCHOR	MADEIRA
U		Light orange	402	1047	2307
	Λ	Very light grey blue	928	900	1709
	−	Pale gold	677	886	2205

*Note: backstitch the border outline in medium golden tan, and the grasses,
ivy leaves, chrysanthemums, fence and bird outlines in dark golden brown.*

35

Winter Landscape Cards

Winter is a time with its own stark beauty. These two delicate landscape pictures, designed to evoke the wintry scene, have been stitched as cards, but they would also make an appealing pair of small pictures.

WINTER LANDSCAPE CARDS

YOU WILL NEED

For each card, measuring 20.5cm × 15cm
(8in × 6in), with a cut-out measuring
14cm × 10cm (5½in × 4in):

*23cm × 17.5cm (9in × 7in) of grey,
28-count Jubilee linen fabric
Stranded embroidery cotton in the colours
given in the panel
No24 tapestry needle
Masking tape
Card with cut-out as specified above (available from
many needlework and craft shops; see also suppliers
listed on page 48)*

*NOTE: if you cannot obtain Jubilee linen, substitute
any other 28-count linen fabric, or use 14-count
Aida; if you are stitching both pictures, you will only
require one skein of each of the colours listed.*

THE EMBROIDERY

For each card, start by preparing the fabric as described on page 4; find the centre by folding, and mark the horizontal and vertical centre lines with basting stitches in a light-coloured thread. Set the fabric in a hoop (see page 5) and count out from the centre to start stitching at a point convenient to you. Use two strands of embroidery cotton in the needle for both cross stitches and half cross stitches, and take each stitch over two threads of the linen fabric. Finish with the backstitching, using one strand of embroidery cotton in the needle.

FINISHING

Remove the basting stitches. Gently handwash the finished embroidery, if necessary, and press lightly on the wrong side. Carefully trim the linen, leaving it approximately 2.5cm (1in) larger than the cut-out each way, and making sure that the design remains centred. Position the embroidery behind the aperture and use masking tape to secure it in place (some cards are self-sealing, in which case you will not require masking tape).

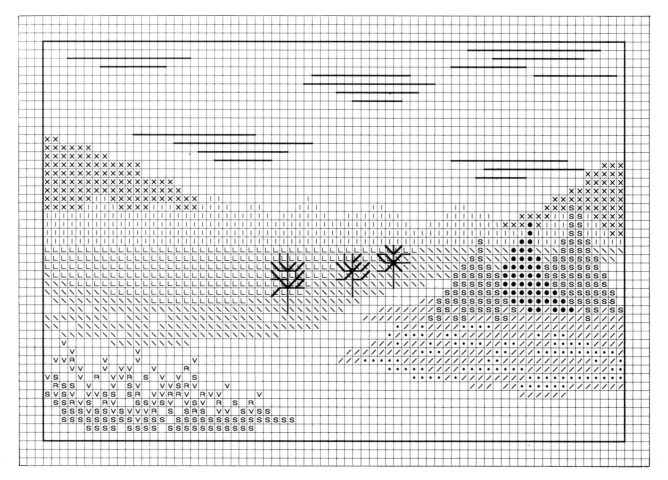

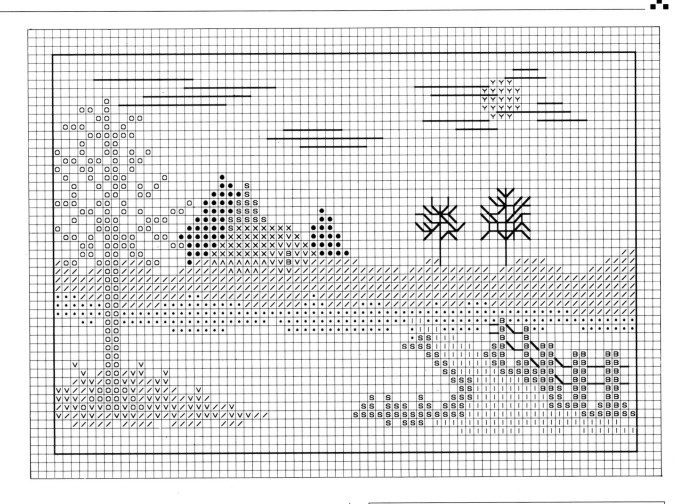

WINTER SUN ▲   DMC ANCHOR MADEIRA

Cross	Half Cross		DMC	ANCHOR	MADEIRA
O		Dark grey brown	640	903	1903
	/	Light grey	415	398	1803
V		Light golden brown	613	831	2109
	•	Very light grey	762	397	1804
●		Dark green	520	862	1514
S		Clear green	3363	262	1602
B		Dark golden brown	611	898	2107
⋀	I	Light brown grey	3023	899	1902
Y		Pale gold	677	882	2205
X		Dark tan brown	433	371	2008
		Dark grey*	414	235	1801
		Very dark golden brown*	610	905	1914
		Light blue grey*	927	849	1708

Note: backstitch the border in dark grey; the trees and fence links in very dark golden brown*, and the lines on the sky in light blue grey* (starred colours are used for backstitch only).*

WINTER LAKE ◀   DMC ANCHOR MADEIRA

Cross	Half Cross		DMC	ANCHOR	MADEIRA
	I	Light brown grey	3023	899	1902
	X	Medium brown grey	3022	392	1903
S		Clear green	3363	262	1602
●		Dark grey	520	862	1514
	/	Light grey	415	398	1803
	•	Very light grey	762	397	1804
R		Light red	3328	1024	0406
V		Medium grey green	522	860	1513
	\	Light golden brown	613	831	2109
	L	Light blue grey	927	848	1708
		Dark grey*	414	235	1801
		Very dark golden brown*	610	905	1914

Note: backstitch the sky in light blue grey; the border in dark grey, and the trees in very dark golden brown* (starred colours are used for backstitch only).*

Winter Blessings

In the foreground of this design, the delicate fragility of a Christmas rose and snowdrops is offset by the brilliance of holly berries. In the background is a cheery robin, and a wintry view of snow-covered hills.

WINTER BLESSINGS

YOU WILL NEED

For the *Winter* picture, set in a mount with a cut-out measuring 12.5cm × 16cm (5in × 6¼in):

*32.5cm × 36cm (13in × 14¼in) of antique white,
18-count Aida fabric
Stranded embroidery cotton in the colours given in
the panel
No26 tapestry needle
Wooden frame measuring 22.5cm × 26cm
(8¾in × 10¼in)
Rectangular mount, cut to fit the frame, with cut-out
as specified above
Strong thread and cardboard, for mounting*

●

THE EMBROIDERY

Prepare the fabric as described on page 4; find the centre by folding, and mark the horizontal and vertical centre lines with basting stitches in a light-coloured thread. Set the fabric in a frame or hoop (see page 5) and count out from the centre to start stitching at a point convenient to you.

One thread of cotton was used in the needle for cross stitches and for backstitch. Work all full cross stitches first, and then the half crosses. The half cross stitches have their own individual symbols on the chart; for each half cross, work only the top stitch of the two that make up a full cross stitch, to produce a more delicate effect.

Take both half and full crosses over one block of the fabric, making sure that all top stitches run in the same direction (if top stitches run in different directions, they will reflect the light in opposite directions and the work will look uneven). Finally, work all backstitch details.

FINISHING

Gently handwash the finished piece, if necessary, and lightly press with a steam iron on the wrong side. Stretch and mount the embroidery as explained on page 6. Insert it into the frame, behind the rectangular mount.

For each of these seasonal pictures, the colour of the mount has been specially selected to echo colours and tones predominant in that particular design, but if you are making them as a set, you might prefer to use one colour for all four.

TOP

WINTER BLESSINGS ▲		DMC	ANCHOR	MADEIRA
Cross Half Cross				
●	Dark blue green	501	878	1704
X	Medium blue green	502	876	1703
V	Light blue green	503	875	1702
B	Dark golden brown	611	898	2107
■	Dark red	349	13	0212
R	Peach red	350	11	0213
·	White	White	2	White
/	Pale cream	712	926	2101
△	Dark olive green	3051	681	1508

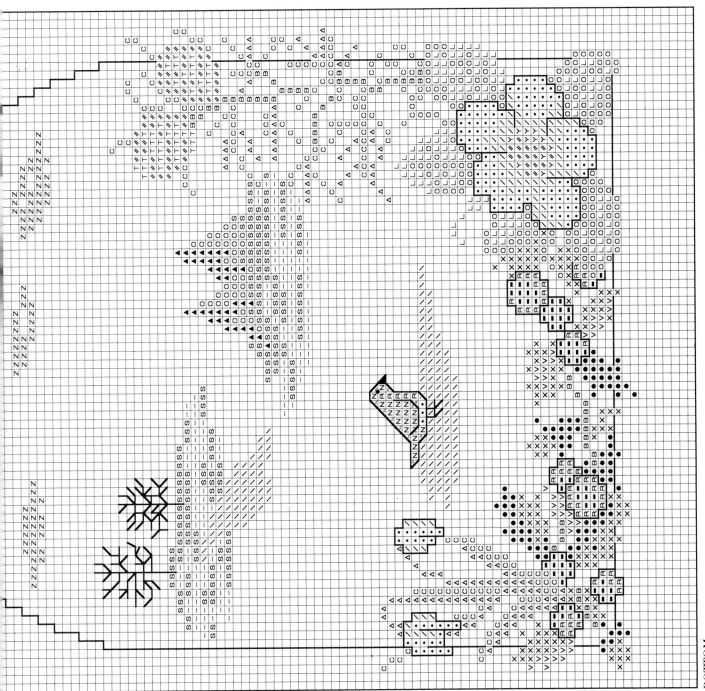

| DMC | ANCHOR | MADEIRA |

Cross	Half Cross		DMC	ANCHOR	MADEIRA
C		Light yellow green	3364	266	1501
O		Clear green	3363	262	1602
L		Light grey green	523	859	1512
∕		Medium golden brown	612	832	2108
Y		Medium yellow	744	301	0112
T		Medium golden tan	420	374	2104
▲		Dark fir green	520	862	1514
	S	Light grey	415	398	1803
	−	Very light grey	762	397	1804

| DMC | ANCHOR | MADEIRA |

Cross	Half Cross		DMC	ANCHOR	MADEIRA
∖		Light golden brown	613	831	2109
N		Medium grey brown	640	903	1905
Λ		Pale gold	677	882	2205
	Z	Pale steel grey	647	1040	1813

Note: backstitch snowdrops in light yellow green, border outline and Christmas rose in dark grey*, and robin, berries and distant trees in dark golden brown* (starred outline colours are used for backstitch only).

43

A Special Time of Year

Christmas stitching remains as popular as ever, and this small seasonal picture will add a festive touch to any home. It would also make a delightful Christmas gift, or you might choose to use the design for a very special Christmas card.

A SPECIAL TIME OF YEAR

For the picture, set in a 12.5cm × 17.5cm
(5in × 7in) frame:

*20cm × 25cm (8in × 10in) of antique white,
28-count Monaco evenweave fabric
Stranded embroidery cotton in the colours given
in the panel
No26 tapestry needle
Strong thread, for lacing
Cross-over wooden frame (for suppliers, see page 48)*

*NOTE: Monaco fabric, from Charles Craft, USA, is
available from many needlework shops and suppliers,
but if you cannot obtain this fabric, use any 28-count
evenweave linen fabric.*

•

THE EMBROIDERY

Prepare the fabric as described on page 4; find the
centre by folding, and mark the horizontal and
vertical centre lines with basting stitches in a light-
coloured thread. Set the fabric in a frame or hoop
(see page 5) and count out from the centre to start
stitching at a point convenient to you.

Work all cross stitching first and then the half
crosses, using two strands of thread in the needle.
Take the stitches over two fabric threads, ensuring
that all top stitches lie in the same direction. Finish
with the backstitching, using one strand of thread in
the needle.

ASSEMBLING THE PICTURE

When the design is completed, gently handwash the
finished piece, if necessary, then press lightly on the
wrong side, using a cool iron. Mark the central
horizontal and vertical lines on the back of the
mount provided and, matching these with the central
basting stitches, lace the embroidery over the
mount, following the instructions on page 6.
Carefully remove the basting stitches.

Insert the embroidery into the frame, according to
the manufacturer's instructions (a framing mount has
not been used with this design).

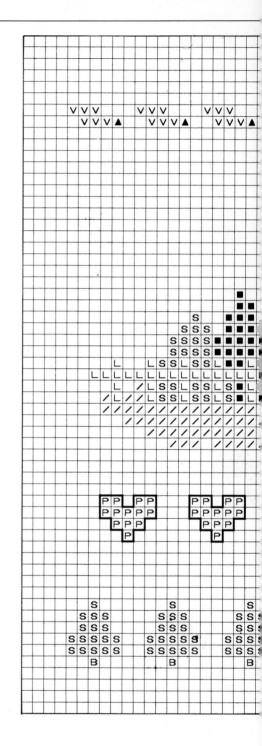

A SPECIAL TIME OF YEAR ▲

Cross	Half Cross		DMC	ANCHOR	MADEIRA
S		Clear green	3363	262	1602
B		Medium golden brown	611	898	2107
P		Medium salmon pink	760	9	0405
▲		Pink red	3328	1024	0406
L		Light golden brown	612	832	2108
■		Dark green	520	862	1514
V		Medium blue green	502	876	1703
I		Dark beige grey	3022	392	1903
T		Light tan brown	437	362	2012
C		Medium brown grey	640	903	1905

Cross	Half Cross		DMC	ANCHOR	MADEIRA
\		Light beige brown	842	376	1910
=		Medium beige grey	3023	899	1902
G		Medium gold	676	891	2208
	/	Pale silver grey	762	397	1804
		Dark golden brown*	610	905	1914

Note: backstitch house outline and window panes in dark golden brown* (used for backstitch only), bow in pink red, and wreath on door in dark green. Use one strand of pink red to make tiny french knots on the wreath on the front door.

47

ACKNOWLEDGEMENTS

This book is dedicated to the memory of Alma, Terry's mother, and also to my dear friends who have added so much to my life – especially Althea and Tersia. You may be far away, but you're still in my thoughts.

The owners of 'Outlines' Picture Framers (22 The Pavement, Clapham Common, London, SW4) did the framing of the four seasonal pictures and 'A Special Time of Year' with their usual friendliness and efficiency. I would also like to thank Mike Grey of Framecraft Miniatures Ltd for supplying the products used for various projects in this book.

SUPPLIERS

The following mail order company has supplied some of the basic items needed for making up the projects in this book:

Framecraft Miniatures Limited
372/376 Summer Lane
Hockley
Birmingham, B19 3QA
England
Telephone: (021) 359 4442

Addresses for Framecraft stockists worldwide
Ireland Needlecraft Pty Ltd
2-4 Keppel Drive
Hallam, Victoria 3803
Australia

Danish Art Needlework
PO Box 442, Lethbridge
Alberta T1J 3Z1
Canada

Sanyei Imports
PO Box 5, Hashima Shi
Gifu 501-62
Japan

The Embroidery Shop
286 Queen Street
Masterton
New Zealand

Anne Brinkley Designs Inc.
246 Walnut Street
Newton
Mass. 02160
USA

S A Threads and Cottons Ltd.
43 Somerset Road
Cape Town
South Africa

For information on your nearest stockist of embroidery cotton, contact the following:

DMC
(also distributors of Zweigart fabrics)

UK
DMC Creative World Limited
62 Pullman Road
Wigston
Leicester, LE8 2DY
Telephone: 0533 811040

USA
The DMC Corporation
Port Kearney Bld.
10 South Kearney
N.J. 07032-0650
Telephone: 201 589 0606

AUSTRALIA
DMC Needlecraft Pty
P.O. Box 317
Earlswood 2206
NSW 2204
Telephone: 02599 3088

COATS AND ANCHOR

UK
Kilncraigs Mill
Alloa
Clackmannanshire
Scotland, FK10 1EG
Telephone: 0259 723431

USA
Coats & Clark
P.O. Box 27067
Dept CO1
Greenville
SC 29616
Telephone: 803 234 0103

AUSTRALIA
Coats Patons Crafts
Thistle Street
Launceston
Tasmania 7250
Telephone: 00344 4222

MADEIRA

UK
Madeira Threads (UK) Limited
Thirsk Industrial Park
York Road, Thirsk
N. Yorkshire, YO7 3BX
Telephone: 0845 524880

USA
Madeira Marketing Limited
600 East 9th Street
Michigan City
IN 46360
Telephone: 219 873 1000

AUSTRALIA
Penguin Threads Pty Limited
25-27 Izett Street
Prahran
Victoria 3181
Telephone: 03529 4400